Personal Growth

MANIFESTING
WITH THE LAW OF
ATTRACTION

MONIQUE JOINER SIEDLAK

Oshun
Publications

Manifesting With the Law of Attraction © Copyright 2017 by Monique Joiner Siedlak

ISBN: 978-1-948834-06-3

All rights reserved

Cover Design by MJS

Cover Image by YAYImages@depositphotos.com

Published by Oshun Publications

www.oshunpublications.com

Contents

Other Books in the Series

Personal and Self Development
Astral Projection for Beginners
Meditation for Beginners
Reiki for Beginners
Manifesting With the Law of Attraction
Stress Management
Time Bound: Setting Your Goals
Healing Animals with Reiki

Want to learn about African Magic, Wicca, or even Reiki while cleaning your home, exercising, or driving to work? I know it's tough these days to simply find the time to relax and curl up with a good book. This is why I'm delighted to share that I have books available in audiobook format.

Best of all, you can get the audiobook version of this book or any other book by me for free as part of a 30-day Audible trial.

Members get free audiobooks every month and exclusive discounts. It's an excellent way to explore and determine if audiobook learning works for you.

If you're not satisfied, you can cancel anytime within the trial period. You won't be charged, and you can still keep your book. To choose your free audiobook, visit:

www.mojosiedlak.com/free-audiobooks

WANT TO BE FIRST TO KNOW?!

JOIN MY NEWSLETTER!

MOJOSIEDLAK.COM/SELF-HELP-AND-YOGA-NEWSLETTER

Introduction

Is there something that you have wanted but don't really know where to start? Have you been dreaming of achieving something, but it has always seemed to be just out of reach? Are you feeling like negativity is taking too much of a role in your life? Are you looking to produce a change in your mindset and become more positive? Are you looking for success at school or work? Do you wish that you could begin to make the money that you have always wanted so that you can live the life that you have always dreamed of? Are you looking for love? Or to mend and strengthen existing relationships? Do you suffer from physical or mental illnesses, and prefer to find a natural way to help manage them? If you identify with any of these things, then manifesting using the Law of Attraction could be the answer you are looking for!

With Rhonda Byrne's The Secret in 2006, the Law of Attraction was launched into the mainstream. Since then, there has been an upsurge of interest in manifesting utilizing the mind's power and the Law of Attraction to create positive change into reality. There have been many books that explain the Law of Attraction. Along with and the many ways to employ it in your life. This book offers an introduction and some helpful tips on beginning your journey into manifesting your hopes and dreams into reality. You will get a short introduction to the basic principles of manifesting and the different areas in your life in which you can use it. One major tool covered is the creation and use of vision boards, which are a primary tool in manifesting the things that you are seeking to bring into your life. There is also a section on celebrity success stories to motivate you and see how successful manifesting can be for those who genuinely believe in its power. One of the great benefits of this book is that it not only focuses on techniques and things that you can do to begin your journey into manifesting, but it also focuses on things not to do as you are working on honing your abilities. After explaining how to remove blocks that may be hindering your success and progress, there is also a section on common mistakes that people make when doing manifestation work. Frequently, mistakes can be the most significant way to learn, so having a section to help you spot mistakes you may encounter is extremely helpful and informative for beginner practitioners. If you believe in the power of your mind and intention, then the Law of Attraction is something that can help you achieve all of your dreams and more. The information in this book can help you to bring all of your dreams and desires into reality.

ONE

What Is Manifesting?

MANIFESTING IS THE BASIC PRINCIPLE OF THE LAW OF Attraction, which can make a change in the outside world by using your thoughts and mind (Shaw, 2014). Many people can make positive things happen just by thinking about them. On the other side of the coin, people can also cause negative things to happen with their mind. The manifesting results are up to you and what type of energy you send out into the world. If you radiate positivity, then good things will come your way. Send out negative vibrations and energy, then it is likely that negative things will follow. If you can change your mindset to reject negative thoughts and build up the ability to think positively, manifesting can significantly influence your life and help you achieve goals that you had only dreamed of before.

How Can Manifesting Make My Dreams a Reality?

Manifest Success

Manifesting is most commonly used for success. Whether that means achieving success at work or in your personal life, manifesting can be the answer to reaching the goals you have set out for yourself in all aspects of your life. Just wishing for general success would be a difficult thing to achieve. Beginning with small successes is good practice and will set you on the right path to the successful life you dream of. In the early stages of your journey in manifesting, it can be easier to focus on small successes instead of larger, long-term goals. While it is good to keep the larger goals in mind, it can be frustrating and counterproductive to only focus on the ultimate goal. For example, if you want to succeed in school, don't just focus on the end goal of earning your degree. Begin by focusing on succeeding on an upcoming test or the success of an upcoming project or presentation. Once you begin to achieve small victories and practice manifesting success, move onto bigger goals like attaining a specific grade in a class. By moving in smaller steps, you will not only come closer to your larger goals, but you will build your confidence. The positive energy that you put out will propel you further towards success. Positive things come to those who put out positive energy, so success is on the horizon. You just need to maintain your focus and know that you will achieve success. The universe will listen if your message is clear.

Manifest Money

Another common desire that people use manifesting to achieve is the desire for money. Manifesting can help with various financial aspects of your life, from ensuring that you pay bills on time, getting a raise, or even receiving an unexpected sum of money (Losier, 2007). Merely saying that you want to be rich is not enough to manifest financial success. This goal is too broad and not specific enough. If one of your financial goals is to have enough money to buy a house, simply wishing for it all at once will most likely be a frustrating experience. How much is the specific house that you want going to cost? Having a more precise number in mind will help you on your journey to success. Begin with smaller goals instead of simply wishing for hundreds of thousands of dollars. First, you could figure out how much of a down payment would be for the house of your dreams and manifest that amount into your life. Having this smaller goal will help push you towards larger successes. With this smaller success under your belt, you will already have part of your goal manifested, and the success of your larger goals will become more tangible. Celebrate your small accomplishments and let them push you towards believing that bigger things will be coming to you in time. Don't allow doubt to creep into your intention. The universe will help you achieve the financial success that you have always wanted.

Manifest Love

There are many different ways that the Law of Attraction can be used to manifest love, including with a significant other, family, and friends (Losier, 2007). Manifesting can be used to find love, but it can also be used to mend relationships and rebuild the love that has been lost or damaged. The great thing about manifesting is that it can work in so many ways and be applied to many different situations. If you are single, you can manifest meeting a love-interest. Maybe you are just seeking a new friendship or expanding your group of friends. Perhaps you want to build a better relationship with your boss or coworkers. Whether it is platonic or romantic love, friendship, or even just positive interactions, manifesting can be an excellent way to attract or build relationships in your life. When you work on putting out positive energy through manifesting, you will attract positive things that can appear in unexpected ways. Even if you are not looking for new friends or already have a significant other, manifesting can also strengthen a bond that you have with someone who is already in your life. If you have lost touch with a close friend, you can use manifesting to bring them back into your life and build an even stronger relationship. The possibilities are endless because it is up to you which relationships you want to develop, keep, and strengthen. While you can't manifest change in others, we often make changes within ourselves and the energy that we put out that attracts positive people into our lives. Keep your energy pure and bright so that it attracts the right kind of people and, if you maintain that light, others will feel its radiant warmth.

Manifest Health

One use of the Law of Attraction that isn't given as much attention is health manifesting. Apart from lowering your stress levels, manifesting can help your body focus on healing and be applied to an endless array of issues (Losier, 2007). Because the Law of Attraction is focused on building positive thoughts and sending out good energy, it can be a huge benefit to your health and wellness. It is often said that constant stress and negativity causes sickness. Based on manifesting principles, putting out constant negative energy will bring negative things back to you. So, regarding health, this can often produce physical ailments or even severe health issues. You could easily be looking to lose some weight, or maybe you have a chronic pain that you hope to manage better. By working towards manifesting positive thoughts and energy, you can improve or maintain your health without intense medical intervention. While you shouldn't avoid medical professionals' help, combining their expertise with your own positive intentions can really help you heal. The body manifests what is in the mind, so radiating positivity can spread throughout your body and give you overall better quality of life. Manifesting can be like meditation. As you focus on positive things and clear your mind of negative thoughts, your stress levels lower. Negative thoughts affecting you physically can be managed, reduced, or even eliminated altogether.

TWO

Creating a Vision Board

VISION BOARDS ARE A VISUALIZATION TECHNIQUE THAT IS A powerful tool used in manifesting dreams and desires. Using a technique similar to scrapbooking and mind-mapping, vision boards are a way to create a physical representation of your inner hopes, dreams, and desires (Morris, 2011). Your vision boards may start out simple, but the more you work with them, the more complex and strongly personal they can become. The more specific your vision board is, the more likely your dreams and goals will become a reality. All you need to create a vision board is a collection of images of your goals, some glue or tape, and some time. Spending time meditating and considering your specific dreams and how they appear in your mind will help you create a more powerful vision board. Imagine your vision board's look and feel before you create a board that matches what you are picturing in your mind. It may not be perfect the first time, but keep trying, and your vision board will become more powerful and attract the kind of success you are seeking.

How Do Vision Boards Help in Manifesting?

Based on the Law of Attraction, the more focus and attention you give to what you want. You visualize that entering into your life, the greater the likelihood that it will come into your life. A critical aspect of using vision boards to manifest your personal desires is to ensure that the imagery is focused and specific. If one of your major goals is to buy a house, use an image representing the style, location, and color of your dream home. Think about details like landscaping or decoration to create an even more specific reflection of your dream house. Try to be as detailed as possible when envisioning the things you desire. The more you focus on the specifics of what you want, the more likely it is that they will be attracted to you. Visualization is a powerful way to train our minds to prepare the rest of our bodies for an experience. Just as an athlete visualizes winning a race or playing a perfect match, we can imagine ourselves achieving success. Having your brain already set on your specific goals and being prepared to achieve success will be easier for you to follow through with the steps you have already visualized. Our mind is wired for repetitive tasks, so repetition is key when trying to build a new skill or habit. When a musician practices a song, they play it repeatedly until their muscle memory can play it without them even having to think about it. The same can be said for visualizing the things that we want. By continually walking through the steps and scenarios of our success, it will be second nature when it comes time to actually live them out, and they will come easily.

How to Create Your Own Vision Board

Collecting Images

Images for your vision board can be gathered from anywhere, including from magazines, books, newspapers, personal photographs, and printouts from your computer. The internet is a vast resource for images and can be a great source to find specific imagery to match your dreams. To really personalize your vision board, meaningful quotes and personal mantras can be added to create an even more engaging experience. Other items such as leaves, pressed flowers, or other found objects can be another great way to make a meaningful and personal vision board that elicits happy thoughts and memories. If you like to draw, then creating a picture of your goal could make for an even more personalized mood board. It is important to ensure that everything on your vision board represents something that you desire and want. Do not post images of what you don't want because this can counteract your intentions. Maintaining a positive focus with your vision board will ensure its success. Make sure that the images that you include on your board really reflect you and your personality. For example, if you have a favorite color that brings you joy; you could create your vision board with that color as a theme or focus. Simple things can really take your vision board to the next level. When you look at your vision board, you want it to elicit a feeling of happiness and positivity so that you manifest positive energy to send out into the universe.

Engaging With Your Vision Board

Once you have created your vision board, place it somewhere visible to engage with it daily. Be sure you spend quality time focusing on your vision board daily or multiple times each day. This is essential because it will continually remind you of the positive goals that you have set. Placing it on your fridge or in an area where you get ready for the day will mean that you have something positive to focus on each time you are in that space. A more recent way that people engage with vision boards is through technology. Setting the vision board as the background of your phone, tablet, or computer can be a great way to continually be reminded of your goals. You are

7

making them a major focus of your day and heightening the likelihood of success. Wherever you choose to place your vision board, make sure it is somewhere that is positive and calming, instead of somewhere where you feel stress. Combining your vision board with a meditation practice can be an excellent way to use it every day. Focus on each part of your vision board during meditation, and it will help you keep focus.

Updating Your Vision Board

As you progress through your journey of manifesting your dreams and desires, the things that you want will change and evolve. Because of your dreams' constant evolution, your vision board will need to change along with them. It is recommended that you create a new vision board once or twice a year. Even if some of your desires stay the same, they may have become more specific. While you can regularly add to your existing vision board, starting fresh every six to 12 months will give a renewed focus and help you maintain a clear and fresh visualization of your goals. Keeping your old vision boards can also be a great way to track your success by giving you a visual reminder of your achievements. If you need motivation, spend some time looking back at the things you have wanted. Concentrate on how successful you have been. Actually seeing a physical representation of your journey can be an excellent way to stay on track.

THREE

How to Manifest Your Dreams with a Negative Significant Other

ONE OF THE MAJOR THINGS HOLDING PEOPLE BACK CAN BE their love life, but this is something that can be overcome by focusing on the desired change. Whether it is a change in the dynamic or a change to the relationship altogether, focusing on manifesting a positive and supportive love life can be the first step in making your dreams a reality. Suppose you feel that your love life or relationship is holding you back from living a positive life or achieving your success. In that case, the following insights can help you make changes to combat negativity. The key is that you can't focus on changing the other person; instead, the focus of change needs to be on yourself. Manifesting does not work on someone else, so wishing for a change in someone else would be a fruitless effort. Instead, focus on what changes you can make within yourself to bring more positivity to the relationship and into your life in general.

Rejecting Negativity

Without any effort, others will be easily affected by your own negativity. This is one of the most important things to get in check when dealing with negative relationships. You must learn to take responsibility for the energy that you are putting out into the world, which can be a hard pill to swallow. Often, in a relationship, we expect our significant other to make changes for the better while failing to take responsibility for the changes that we, ourselves, need to make. Work to reject negativity and focus on putting positive energy out into the world. When we make small changes in ourselves, it can be surprising how large others' positive changes can be.

Managing Expectations

Manifesting can be a double-edged sword because it can also cause negativity while it can bring positive change. If you constantly believe that you will have a negative or harmful interaction with someone, that will be more likely to occur because you have been manifesting it. While you may not be able to manifest the actions of another person, you can successfully manifest your own interactions with someone by managing expectations and radiating positivity. Don't expect change to happen right away, either. You need to have patience when manifesting and working with the Law of Attraction. The more you practice, the easier it will become, and the faster you will begin to see results. Just as you can't expect someone else to change overnight, the changes you need to make within yourself won't happen right away, either.

Focusing On Yourself

As you reject negativity and begin to take responsibility for the energy you are putting out, realize that this is only the first step in dealing with a negative relationship or significant other. While it may seem that others need to change to ensure your happiness, it is actually you that needs to make the most change. Instead of worrying about how others are making you feel, focus on how you are making yourself feel. It is extremely common for people to find happiness in external forces or other people's energy. So concentrate on yourself and taking responsibility for your own emotions can be a difficult change to make. Changing a habit takes practice, so work on it and take time out to spend time alone to focus on yourself. Practice sending out positive energy and vibrations into the universe. You will begin to see changes happening within yourself and with others. The changes might not happen right away, but keep practicing, and what you put out into the world will begin to come back to you in unexpected ways. Spending time getting to know yourself will significantly impact your relationships as you are putting out positive vibrations and energy.

Giving & Receiving

It can be so easy to blame our unhappiness on the actions of others. Still, as we learn to focus on ourselves and take responsibility for our actions and feelings, the positivity spreads. If you feel a lack of love and respect from a partner, you can focus on respecting and loving yourself and you will begin to receive it from others. In the same way that people say to treat others the way you want to be treated, treat yourself the way you want others to treat you. Instead of waiting for affirmations from others, give them to yourself, and others will follow. Positive energy is infectious, which means that the more you put out, the more you will receive in return.

Letting Go

While this is often one of the last options that need to be considered, sometimes it is best to let a person go if their negativity is too much of an influence on your life. Even though letting go will be hard initially, the benefits will soon start to appear, and positivity will begin to overtake the negativity that has been dominating that aspect of your life. Make sure to focus on the positive aspects of your new life away from negative people. Instead of focusing on how alone you may feel, think about how much free time you have to pursue new interests or revisit old ones. Instead of wondering what the other person is doing without you; focus on the positive things you will be able to do. Manifest new positive things to replace the empty space that is inevitable when you let someone go out of your life. As time moves on and you work on manifesting new and positive experiences, the negative memories will fade away. The new exciting life that you have manifested will begin to unfold.

FOUR

Removing Those Blocks

WHEN YOU ARE MANIFESTING WITH THE LAW OF ATTRACTION, it can be challenging to maintain a clear mind to ensure that you send out positive energy and vibrations into the world. Manifesting can work both ways. Attracting both positive and negative energy. It is crucial to your success in managing negative thoughts and feelings during your practice. Many people put lots of effort into creating vision boards or repeating affirmations daily but never see any results. Unless you can manage negative thoughts and work to remove blocks, all the positive energy you put into the world will be unable to manifest into the things you have been hoping for. Learning all of the manifesting techniques is essential, but learning ways to block the negative energy that inhibits manifesting is equally important. The following methods can not only lower your stress and improve your physical health, but they can make way for your positive energy to flow freely and come back to you in the form of your hopes and dreams. You don't need to use all of the techniques together, but choose ones that work and feel right for you. You will be well on your way to successfully manifesting using the Law of Attraction.

Affirmations and Mantras

Affirmations and personal mantras are a great way to stay motivated and keep your internal talk positive. A mantra is a word or phrase that can create transformation (The Big Book of Personal Affirmations and Mantras, 2011). They can be as simple as "you can do it." Still, often generic or straightforward affirmations lose their power over time and are not as effective. It is best to have a deeply personal and well-constructed phrase or set of phrases that hold a special significance for you. While you can start with a simple phrase to get you going, spend time developing a set of phrases that are personal and meaningful. To create a personal mantra or affirmation, you need to recognize the areas with which you struggle. Is your internal dialogue negative? Does it prevent you from trying new things or putting yourself out there? If this is the case, your mantra could be focused on affirming your ability to try new things and telling yourself how capable you really are. Do you lack confidence in your day-to-day life? Then you need to develop a mantra focused on confidence and your ability to succeed in the situations that challenge you. Do you find yourself lacking motivation and unable to complete tasks or stay focused enough to follow through with your plans? Your mantra will need to be focused on motivation if you want to overcome this type of issue. The great thing about mantras and personal affirmations is that they can be applied to such a broad array of situations. Whatever you struggle with or whatever is blocking your ability to manifest positive things, a mantra focused on the specific block you are dealing with could be the answer to improving your ability to use the Law of Attraction.

Exercise and Yoga

Many people think that exercise is just a way to stay fit and active. People feel similarly about yoga, which is seen as just a way to stretch and improve flexibility. People fail to realize that exercise and yoga have more benefits than just a simple way to stay active. Meditative practice, such as yoga, can generate and distribute healing energy throughout the body (Wörle & Pfeiff, 2010). Whether you are facing a physical or mental ailment, meditative exercise can help you to send healing energy to the parts of your body and specific cells that require healing. As with other methods of removing blocks, exercise and yoga are excellent because they are so customizable. Yoga, for example, can be modified to any ability level. If you have physical limitations, simpler poses can be used to both improve your flexibility and produce the healing energy needed to remove blocks. It can also help you to manifest health into your body and life. Exercise can be an extremely gratifying way to remove blocks because it gives a sense of satisfaction when completed. Knowing that you have put in the effort and spent time working towards a goal gives a sense of accomplishment that can have a lasting positive effect. Exercise and yoga can be an excellent way to start off the day because it will set you off on the right foot. Knowing that you have completed the task will start off your day with having already achieved something great. As you move through the day, you can remind yourself of the great work you have already done, helping you go forward and maintain a positive mindset.

Meditation

Meditation is another excellent tool to remove blocks because it is so simple. You don't need any equipment, special training, or even a specific space in which to practice it. Meditation can be done by anyone anywhere (Bodian, 2006). All you really need to meditate is to find a quiet place where you can get comfortable. It is a great idea to set up a special area in your home where you feel the calmest. Somewhere with nice lighting and good energy works best, but which space you use is up to your individual preference. To begin meditation, you need to close your eyes, take a few deep, controlled breaths, and relax your body as much as you can. It is best to mentally explore each area of your body and focus on relaxing that specific area before moving on. As you settle into your relaxed state, focus on one particular sound, or saying. This is a great way to use your mantras and personal affirmations. As you continue your controlled breathing, repeat your mantra or personal affirmation, and try to keep your mind clear of outside thoughts. If your mind begins to wander, reset, and begin again. The more you practice, the more natural and easy meditation will become for you. To begin, start with about five minutes or so. Still, as you get more practice and can maintain focus, you can extend your meditation sessions. When you have finished your meditation, open your eyes, and stand up slowly. Stretch your hands above your head and then reach down towards your feet. Roll your shoulders back a few times and stretch any parts of your body that feel tight. Even if you take five minutes to begin or end your day, or if you need to practice meditation to calm yourself throughout the day, this is a very useful tool to reset your mind and refocus on positivity.

Reiki

Reiki is a holistic form of hands-on healing that is based in Eastern medicine. The direct translation of the word Reiki is "universal life force" (Malone, 2018). Since Reiki is all about energy and modifying your energy to heal, it pairs well with manifestation. Not only does Reiki help you to clear away all the negative energy that can block your manifesting efforts, but it can enhance the positive energy that you are putting out and make your manifesting more powerful. Practicing Reiki on yourself involves placing the hands on various parts of the body, and breathing deeply and intentionally. As you breathe, focus your hands' energy into relaxing the specific area of the body that you are engaging with. You can use Reiki in your meditation practice, or use it alone to relax and reset your intentions. A great way to employ Reiki in manifesting is to write something that you are trying to manifest on a small piece of paper. Place the paper between your hands and focus the same energy that you would onto your own body in self-practice onto the piece of paper. Breathe deeply as you focus on what you wrote on the paper. Push positive energy from your hands into the physical representation of what you hope to manifest. This method can make it easier to focus on manifesting a specific thing because you have created a physical version of your desire. Instead of thinking about an abstract concept, this method allows you to focus on something physical that is much easier for your mind to maintain its focus on. Although you can practice Reiki techniques alone, removing blocks and having success with manifesting can also be done when you have someone else performing Reiki on you. Spend time making a connection and letting them know about the things that you are hoping to manifest. They can help to manipulate your energy towards making the change that you desire. It is best to find a reiki practitioner with whom you have a strong connection, so keep looking until you find the right person. Listen to your gut. You will know when the right person comes along to help you reach your goals and remove blocks that prevent you from manifesting successfully.

Detoxing

Sometimes manifestations can be blocked by not only one's mind but by physical influences as well. While many people wouldn't consider it a significant influence, your diet can significantly impact the energy you are putting out. In the same way that putting negative energy out into the world can bring back negativity, putting bad and unhealthy foods into your body can cause you to exude negativity. While unintentional, the negative energy that is being put out because of your diet can impact your efforts to manifest positive things. Your body naturally filters toxins that you ingest. Yet, sometimes when you are continually eating bad foods, there can be a build-up of negativity in your system. Controlled detoxification of your body can be a great way to reset your body and work towards a more positive existence (Jacobs, 2010). While there are so many different detox plans out there, the key is to be intentional about what you are putting into your body and avoid overly-processed foods. Instead of eating lots of fat-heavy and sugar-filled foods, focus on eating whole and natural foods.

Another thing that can affect the food you are putting into your body is how it is prepared. If you are cooking with negative energy, such as anger, the same energy put into the making of your food will be put into your body. This means refocusing your intentions when preparing food and having a more positive mindset. Work towards enjoying cooking instead of resenting it, since the energy you put into making your food will be what is, in turn, put into your body. Prepare your food with love and positive intentions. You will begin to notice that your relationship with food and eating will become more positive, positively affecting your energy overall.

Enjoying Nature

Many of the techniques discussed so far are things that you practice inside and in your own house, making it easy to forget that there is a calming force all around us—nature! While it is great to explore new places, it can be just as helpful to revisit your favorite natural space regularly. You will quickly notice how much variation occurs within the same space, and, as you get to know your favorite area, it will reveal more to you each time. Nature feeds off of our energy, so making sure to explore nature with positivity and love is key to removing blocks and negativity from your mind. The presence of animals is a sure sign that the space is getting to know and trust you. Be aware of your surroundings and look for signs of life that trust you enough to reveal themselves. When exploring nature, make sure to respect the space and as little impact on the ecosystem as possible. It is okay to take a few token items like a stone or flower, but it is best to leave natural spaces undisturbed. A great way to enjoy nature intentionally is by employing a mindfulness technique and apply it to your time spent outside. This mindfulness technique helps you focus your mind positively and consciously enjoy your surroundings, which can develop a tremendous positive energy that you can then put into your manifestation techniques. Focus your attention on where you are and explore the space with your five major senses.

First, find five things that you can see and focus on each of them more deeply. Second, find five things that you can touch. Third, find five things that you can hear. Fourth, find five things that you can smell. Finally, find five things that you can taste. Spending the time to see all of these things in the space you are in will make you explore your surroundings with more intention and appreciate nature more deeply. Depending on the space you are in, it may be difficult to find five things to smell, taste, and hear, so the exercise can be modified to make it easier. Start with five things that you see and, with each sense, find one less thing so that you will only end up needing to find one thing to taste. This will make your exploration a bit easier but still have the same positive effect.

FIVE

Most Common Mistakes in Manifesting

MANY BOOKS ON MANIFESTING GIVE YOU MANY DIFFERENT techniques to make your dreams and desires a reality. However, they don't often include the mistakes you are trying to manifest. While all the techniques that you can learn are extremely valuable, mistakes are often just as useful to learn. The following are a few of the most basic mistakes to look for when working towards manifesting. Suppose you can catch these before they become a habit. In that case, your journey towards attracting positivity and manifesting the things you desire will be much easier, and you will see results faster. As you learn and practice, be aware of your mistakes but don't get bogged down in them. Look at your mistakes as a learning experience, since mistakes often provide the best lessons. Just make sure that you remain aware and move past the mistakes to heighten your success.

Not Taking Action

Your goals are not manifesting because you are focused too much on believing that the end goal will just happen out of the blue. When you are trying to manifest your dreams, you have to learn when to employ action. Sometimes, simply believing that something will happen is not enough to really make the Law of Attraction work for you. Sending positive energy out into the world through action can be just as powerful and sometimes even more powerful than intentional thinking alone. As you work towards manifesting your goal, you have to listen to your intuition when it tells you to take action and do something. While these actions may not seem like they have anything to do with your end goal, the universe may be working strangely and mysteriously to push you towards your end goals. Instead of overthinking your feeling of wanting to take action or second-guess your intuition, go with your gut and follow the path that your mind, body, and soul want to take.

Not Sticking With What You Send Out

When working with the Law of Attraction, it is essential to maintain focus and not let your mind be filled with too many wants or desires. If you start sending out chaotic thoughts and a mess of different things that you want the universe to give you, a confusion of results will be thrown back at you. When you don't stick with what you send out, so many different things can come about that they may cancel each other or go unnoticed because of your lack of focus. When you are beginning to work with the Law of Attraction, make sure that the goal you choose is something that you really want and is not just a passing phase. If you continually change your manifestation practice's primary goal, you will likely not see any results. Maintain the same focus every day and make manifesting the same thing part of your daily routine. While goals and desires may change or evolve over time, it is important to stick with your dream's main essence instead of letting your imagination run wild. Make sure that the message you are sending out to the universe is clear so that the results and messages you receive back are just as clear. Stick with what you send out, and the results will come to you in time.

Anticipating Instant Results

A major mistake that people make when they are beginning to work with the Law of Attraction is expecting instant results. As with all things, manifesting takes a lot of patience. If you are always thinking that your dreams and desires just aren't happening quickly enough, that message is actually part of the message and energy you are sending out into the universe. When the energy you send out consists of mixed messages, it is hard for your desired results to manifest correctly. By continually focusing on the fact that your desire has yet to arrive, you actually counteract the original message, and it can take even longer for results to materialize. When you catch yourself having these counteractive thoughts, take some time to reset your intentions so that the universe hears your desires loud and clear. Tell yourself and the universe that you are willing to be patient and accept the things you are trying to manifest at any time that the universe can provide them. It is up to you to manage your expectations and avoid trying to rush things into existence. Even if you have to tell yourself to be patient as part of your daily manifesting practices, this can signal to the universe you are trying. As long as the intention is positive. After all, good things come to those who wait!

You Hope It Will Work

Simply hoping that what you ask for will happen is not enough to really see results from manifesting. For manifesting and the Law of Attraction to work, you have to be sure that it will work. One of the essential aspects of the practice of manifesting is a true belief that it is real and will work in your life. If your belief is wavering or you are having doubts about the process, those things will be sent out with all of the things you are attempting to manifest. Having a firm belief in the Law of Attraction is one of the main ways to ensure that it works. If you begin to feel yourself doubting the process or your belief is wavering, it is time to reset your intentions and refocus your energy. Figure out what first drew you to manifesting and the Law of Attraction, and what sparked your interest. Suppose you have had little or no results with manifesting. In that case, it can be hard to stay on track, and it becomes very easy to continually focus on the hope that it will work. Try not to confuse the message you are sending out, and instead of hoping that manifesting will work, you have to know that it will work.

Limiting the Universe

Thoughts limiting the universe can be difficult to spot because they are often so ingrained in our minds that we don't even realize that we have them. Frequently, these thoughts are something that directly counteracts the thing that we are trying to manifest. Whether we know it or not, our core beliefs are part of the energy that we are sending out. So understanding whether you have any that counteract your desires is important in succeeding in manifesting things you want. If one of the major things that you are trying to manifest is a new car because you would love to stop having to take the bus back and forth from work, there could be a core belief that is preventing a car from being manifested into your life. If you believe that cars are polluting the earth or are just a money-pit, then these beliefs limit the universe from giving you the car you have been asking for. Suppose you are trying to manifest a good grade on an upcoming essay, but you have a core belief that you aren't good at writing. In that case, the ingrained thought is neutralizing what you are asking for. When you decide on something to manifest, do some searching within yourself to ensure that you don't have any beliefs that might counteract your desires. If you find something that doesn't quite match up, then you may need to put in a bit of extra effort to change your core ideas so that your journey into manifesting is successful.

Not What You Expected

Expectations are a major aspect of manifesting that people don't give enough attention to. Suppose you are trying to manifest something but have the expectation that it won't happen. In that case, the outcome will match your expectation. No matter how much you try to manifest it into existence. If you expect that you will fail a class, for example, no matter how hard you try to manifest passing grades on assignments and tests, they just won't happen. Your expectations don't match your desires. So if the class is a prerequisite for another course being offered in the next semester, don't wait until you find out your grade to register. Sign up for the class because you are expecting that you are going to pass the current one. You can't just sit around waiting for something to come along and change your expectations; your expectations need to be changed to match what you want to happen. If you are looking for a new couch but just can't find one you like, maybe your expectations don't match what you are trying to manifest. Rearrange your living room to make space for the couch that you are expecting. All the energy that you put into wanting something to come into your life adds to the intentions that the universe is receiving from you. To ensure that your intentions manifest, make sure that your expectations match.

Not Paying Attention

If you aren't paying attention to the universe, then it is likely that the universe is having trouble paying attention to you too. Sometimes your focus can become so narrow that you develop blinders and fail to notice all the gifts and signs that the universe is actually giving to you. To be successful at manifesting your desires, it is important to remain aware of signals from the universe. Use your intuition and pay attention to the signs that the universe is trying to give you. Often, signs that your manifestation is well on its way to coming into your life appear in repetition. The universe is pretty persistent when it is trying to tell you something, so don't worry too much that you will miss it. Remain aware of your surroundings and look for things that seem out of the ordinary. Are you frequently seeing the same number come up in your day-to-day life? Are events and other things in your life lining up a bit too perfectly? People can easily brush these things off as coincidence. Still, it is, in fact, the universe trying to tell you that it has heard your intentions and is on its way to fulfilling them. Believe in these signs, and the universe will know that you are ready to receive the things you are asking for. Stay aware of your surroundings at all times because you never know when the universe might be trying to tell you something.

Becoming Impatient

Sometimes, as you become impatient, waiting for the things you want to manifest, the energy you start to send out isn't always positive. Feelings of frustration and anxiety can severely affect the energy and vibrations you send out and mask your true intentions. It is important to keep your thoughts pure and focus on as much positivity as you can. Like how people expect instant results, the message you are sending out can be modified and confused by your impatience. While it is important to maintain focus on the things you are trying to manifest, you sometimes need to listen to your gut and modify your desires. It may not mean changing your focus altogether, but perhaps you just need to think of what you want in a new way. By changing your intention's direction, you can come to the same desire from another angle and with a renewed vision. Be patient with the universe. When you start to let negative or uncertain feelings seep in, your manifestations' focus is not received with enough clarity for them to happen the way you want.

SIX

Celebrities and the Law of Attraction

MANY PEOPLE FIND SUCCESS THROUGH THE USE OF manifesting techniques and the Law of Attraction. While many of those people are regular, everyday people, many celebrities speak openly about their belief in the Law of Attraction. Just remember that celebrities were once people like you and me before their rise to fame. By seeing how celebrities manifested their success, it can be easier to envision your own achievements. The following success stories and quotes can serve as inspiration as you begin your journey into using the Law of Attraction for your benefit. It is important to maintain a strong belief in the process as you work towards your goal. If you find your belief or motivation wavering, think of these success stories to keep you on track. If this diverse group of celebrities can manifest their success, so can you!

Jim Carrey

Jim Carrey is an award-winning Canadian-American actor and comedian. He has been appearing in television and film since the early 1980s. Carrey was born in the Toronto suburb of Newmarket into a lower middle-class, Roman Catholic family. He has become one of the top fifty highest-grossing actors in North American film throughout his forty-year career. While he is best known for his role in films like The Mask (1994), Ace Ventura: Pet Detective (1994), and The Truman Show (1998), he has appeared in over forty feature films throughout his career. Besides his extensive career in film and television, he is also known for his work as an artist, author, writer, and producer. Carrey often speaks about his belief in the Law of Attraction and considers manifesting to be the reason he is where he is today. His family struggled financially during his early life, and he believes manifesting to be the reason for his rise to fame and success. Jim Carrey had the following to say about his experience with manifesting an interview with Oprah Winfrey:

"As far as I can tell, it's just about letting the universe know what you want and then working towards it while letting go of how it comes to pass" (Carrey, as cited in Hurst, 2019).

Lady Gaga

Born in New York City as Stefani Germanotta, Lady Gaga rose to fame with smash hits 'Just Dance' and 'Poker Face' from her 2007 debut album The Fame. While initially known as a singer, songwriter, and pianist, she has more recently received critical acclaim for her acting. In between writing and recording her six full-length albums, Gaga has toured extensively and wowed an audience of millions with her 2017 Super Bowl halftime show. In 2018, Gaga was thrust further into the spotlight with her acclaimed performance in A Star Is Born (2018) alongside Bradley Cooper. For her acting in the film and contributions to the soundtrack, Lady Gaga won an Oscar, Grammy, BAFTA award, and a Golden Globe. From her humble beginnings growing up in New York, Lady Gaga has achieved worldwide success and is beloved by millions.

She attributes much of her success to believing that she would accomplish all that she has and using affirmations to manifest all that she had hoped, dreamed, and more. In an interview with Anderson Cooper, Gaga had the following to say about her experience using affirmations and the Law of Attraction to manifest her success and fame:

"It's sort of like a mantra. You repeat it to yourself every day. 'Music is my life. Music is my life. The fame is inside of me, I'm going to make a number one record with number one hits.' And it's not yet, it's a lie. You're saying a lie over and over and over again, and then, one day, the lie is true" (Germonatta, as cited in Hurst, 2019).

Denzel Washington

Denzel Washington is an American actor born in Mount Vernon, New York, in 1954 to a Pentecostal Minister and a beauty shop owner. While he began acting in the late 1970s, his first major role was in the medical drama, St. Elsewhere, which ran from 1982 to 1988. Since the beginning of his acting career, Washington has appeared in numerous television shows, stage productions, and over fifty feature-length films. He is best known for his roles in movies, such as Glory (1990), Malcolm X (1993), The Hurricane (2000), and Training Day (2002). He is the recipient of multiple awards for his acting, including two Oscars, two Golden Globes, and a Tony Award. While many of his youth's peers ended up following paths of crime, Washington always strived for success. He has spoken openly about his belief that you receive back what you put out into the world, which is a primary principle in the Law of Attraction. He had the following to say on the subject:

"Positively and negatively, you attract what you feel, you attract who you are, you attract what you attract" (Washington, as cited in Hurst, 2019).

Arnold Schwarzenegger

Arnold Schwarzenegger, who was born in Austria and moved to the United States of America at the age of 21, is an actor, businessman, former professional bodybuilder, and served as the governor of California between 2003 and 2006. Schwarzenegger began pursuing bodybuilding seriously as a teenager. By the time of his final retirement from the sport at the age of 33, he had won first place in nineteen competitions, including Mr. Europe, Mr. Universe, and Mr. Olympia. In the 1970s, Schwarzenegger achieved his dream of working in the film industry as an actor and would act in almost fifty films and numerous television series and work as a video game voice actor. Schwarzenegger is best known for his roles in The Terminator franchise, which began with the film Terminator in 1984, Conan the Barbarian (1982), Total Recall (1990), Junior (1994), Jingle All The Way (1996), and many more. Schwarzenegger has said many times that you have to believe in what you want to achieve. It will happen if you continue to put the ideas into the universe, which is one of the key concepts behind manifesting and the Law of Attraction. He revealed the following about his experience visualizing his success:

"When I was very young, I visualized myself being and having what it was I wanted. Mentally, I never had any doubts about it" (Schwarzenegger, as cited in Hurst, 2019).

Oprah Winfrey

Oprah Winfrey, a talk-show host, actor, producer, author, businesswoman, and philanthropist who has become one of the most recognizable women in American culture, was born to an unmarried teenage mother in rural Mississippi. Her childhood was not an easy one. She lived in poverty and faced abuse, neglect, and gave birth to a child at the age of fourteen, who unfortunately died soon after being born prematurely. Winfrey began her television career as a news anchor in the late 1970s and quickly shifted to hosting talk shows. By 1986, she had earned producers' attention and began The Oprah Winfrey Show, which quickly became the top talk show in the United States. Over the next thirty years, Winfrey's popularity grew. Her show was beloved by millions of devoted fans by the time it finished airing in 2011. Since then, her empire has only grown to include a magazine, television network, book club, and countless other successful ventures. In an interview with Larry King, Winfrey discusses her use of the Law of Attraction long before it became mainstream in the mid-2000s. Speaking about manifesting her role in the 1985 film, The Color Purple, Winfrey said the following:

"The way you think creates reality for yourself" (Winfrey, as cited in Hurst, 2019).

Steve Harvey

Steve Harvey is an American comedian, actor, entertainer, author, radio host, and television host who has been working in the entertainment industry since the 1980s. Born in West Virginia and having worked in various positions such as a mailman, an autoworker, and a carpet cleaner, he began his comedy career performing at clubs in 1985. During this time, he struggled to make ends meet and was homeless for about three years. After slowly growing in popularity, he began working as a television host and appeared in television comedies. In 1996, he was the host of his own talk show, The Steve Harvey Show, which ran until 2002. Since then, he has made numerous appearances and has become best-known for hosting the game-show Family Feud since 2010. He also has his own morning radio show that has been airing since 2000. Harvey is a huge fan of the Law of Attraction and promoted The Secret (2006) on his television show. He attributes his success to the belief that the universe will give back what you put out into it, a central concept behind the Law of Attraction. He had the following to say about his experiences with this type of manifestation:

"You are a magnet. Whatever you are, that's what you draw to you. If you're negative, you're going to draw negativity. If you're positive, you're going to draw positivity" (Harvey, as cited in Hurst, 2019).

SEVEN

Law of Attraction Stories

Anna's Story

ANNA HAD BEEN A SINGLE MOM FOR TEN YEARS, AND throughout that time, she went through a few unsuccessful relationships. She had always desired a special relationship, but couldn't find it. Anna had her heart broken a few times, however instead of giving up; she depicted precisely to her sister, what she needed her guy to be like as well as writing down whom she felt her ideal relationship and partner was. With the complete belief that one day she would find him, Anna then let it go. A month later, she literally ran into her now husband during a 5K race.

Danny's Story

Around a year ago, Danny wanted to get a new job, but he had such conditions as he sought a job that was about half an hour away from his home since he did not like to travel. Next, Danny wanted Saturday and Sunday off and it should be in a business office since he had always been working in the hospitality industry.

Danny received many job offers however, none matched in his terms and he was nonchalant about it. Many times while sitting at his window, Danny used to look at individuals waiting for the bus as they headed to their own office. It then dawned on him that even he ought to travel on the bus that was going to the same building that used to come into his mind.

After two months, Danny unexpectedly got a call for a job interview. He did not know who he was and how he got his number but mysteriously, Danny got the job precisely in the area close to his home. Danny had been looking for Saturday and Sunday off in a respectable corporate office and he is now traveling on the bus, as he wanted to. It was like magic. After eight months, he says he is happy working there.

Jacki's Story

Jacki was one of many striving for a limited position in a very competitive nursing program in Florida. She had done the required educational and other work necessary and applied with many others. Her friends would say, "What if I don't get in?" or "I hope I get in!" They were going to worry until the time they heard back. Jacki would ask the Universe and imagined that she got a spot in the program. She did not worry about it for the reason that Jacki believed that it was already decided that she was one of the chosen.

Jacki went about her days and had the belief and feeling that she was already in the program. She made an in depth financial and other plans that were necessary as if she was already chosen to be in the yearlong program. Jacki went on vacation with her family. When she came back, her acceptance letter was waiting for her. That was over a year ago.

As an update, Jacki not long ago applied to the subsequent phase in her career path. She applied for the next program that has equally driven and low percentage of acceptance into. This time she says it was even easier! Jacki deliberated and asked to get into this program, and with the absolute belief that it was already decided and that she was already going to be in, and planned her life as if it was already decided. Once again, she was accepted into that program.

Brittany's Story

Back in 2010, Brittany had started a new position at a real estate firm. Not long after that, she was reading books on the Law of Attraction and began focusing on a dream car she loved.

Brittany had written herself a check and deposit slip for $30,000.00 dated December 1st and began her search for her dream car. She even went as far as showing her husband a picture of her new car that she taped to her bathroom mirror. He asked her how she planned to pay for it. Brittany explained that she already had the check and deposit slip written.

In September, she acquired a client that a coworker could not handle because of a family emergency. It turned out to be the quickest real estate sales transaction to date of the business.

Brittany closed that deal two weeks later and November 30th, she made a deposit of $32,000.00 in her checking account. It was an excellent early Christmas present.

My Stories

How I Bought My Home

About ten years ago, all I wanted was a house of my own for me and my children. I worked sometimes two jobs. When the time came that I felt I was ready, I found the house I wanted. I was ecstatic! A brand new house! I copied the floor plans and could see where everything would go. How the rooms would be painted. Everything.

Then, the housing market crashed. The mortgage I ended up qualifying for was thirty thousand less than the previous week. I did not have another thirty thousand. Talk about being heartbroken. I cannot describe it. Therefore, I squared my shoulders, got my head right. I worked and saved as much as I can.

A friend of mine at work said, "Girl, you got this. You can get a house on your own. You do not need anybody." Boy was he right.

Two months later, I saw a flyer posted in the grocery store. I was intrigued and went to see the realtor. The first house she showed me was the same model I had my heart on. Not only that, it was forty thousand less. Not only did I get the exact house I wanted, it was in a neighborhood closer to my job and I did not have to put any money down. After decorating the house with paint and furniture, I still had plenty of money left for a healthy rainy day fund.

My Husband

Almost a year and a half after buying my house, I felt the need to start dating again. My only problem was that all I did was work. It was just something I did. I joined many dating sites and most of them really thought I was just some desperate woman. Not! I also fell in love with the movie Something New. I watched that movie at least three times a week. I saw myself as the lead actress. We were both workaholics. After six months, I decided to shut down all my accounts. I was ready to give up. The following evening I saw a commercial for eHarmony's free nights and weekends on Memorial Day and it was the last night. Since it was free, I thought I would try it. After answering all their questions, I was matched with someone whose screen name was Ziggy. Of course, I thought about the comics. We messaged each other back and forth for about an hour until he said that he had to go. I asked him if he had to walk his dog. He said yes. Now mind you, I never asked him if he had a dog. Since it was the last night, he asked for my email address so he could get back in touch with me, so I did. A week later, I never hear from him. Figured he was another person attempting to play me. The Fourth of July I spent with a friend of mine who I not only worked with, but also lived right down the street. She had a fractured kneecap, so I kept her company and ran her errands. When I got home that night, I went to do some work on my computer and realized I had not cleaned my files in a long time. I was about to delete all my junk mail when something said to check it. In my junk mail were emails from him. How and why they ended up there, we will never know. Once we finally met, it was love at first sight. We decided to get married two months later. Oh, and he did have a dog.

My Husband's Truck

After getting my house and then my husband, I decided to go all out on a vision board. It was actually my first time hearing about one. I knew we were going to Europe the following year, so I began to place pictures of the countries I would like to go. All of Europe you might say. I also decided it was time to get another car. There was nothing wrong with my Honda Odyssey. I had it for over eleven years, but I was down to one child needing me to drive her around town. I found a picture of a grey 2011 New Beetle. Something I wanted for the future.

Not long after, my husband's truck began acting up and I asked him what type of truck he was looking for. He wanted an SUV instead of another pickup. I began looking online at dealerships not only in our area, but the surrounding areas as well. I saw one and thought it looked like something he might want and printed it. A few days later, there was an SUV in our driveway. Not only that, it was the exact one I printed from the dealer. My husband didn't believe me until he actually saw it on my vision board. The dealership was in a neighboring county and I've never been there before.

My Favorite Car

My husband left Poland in 1981 and hadn't been back. For our first anniversary, we went to Europe to see his Dad. Our rental from Frankfurt was a grey 2010 beetle. I was totally amped. It was a year older. After driving through Germany, Poland and the Czech Republic, I knew this was to be.

When we returned home, I mentioned again how we ended up with the same type of car that was on my vision board. After that, my trusty car decided to act up. Did she know I wanted to replace her? As long as I had my car, the check engine light never came on. I took her in and ended up with a $500. repair bill. A week later, it started acting up again. I wasn't going to take it back in. I figured it was time to find another. My only problem was I didn't come across any Beetle that said "Here I am!" Maybe because it had to be a manual. I was about to give up when a Sunset Orange KIA Rio popped up. It felt right, so I purchased it. I enjoyed driving a smaller vehicle with a stick.

I drove my husband's SUV a few months later to get groceries on a day I was off and he had to go to work. I was just putting everything away when he called and said he was in an accident. Someone in a large SUV drove him off the road. Apparently, he couldn't see that bright orange car. Needless to say, the Kia was totaled. As we went to collect all my effects from the Kia, we passed a Volkswagen dealership and my husband noticed a blue beetle. We decided to stop there on our way back, but we did. Fingers crossed it was a manual transmission. It was love at first sight. After adding racing stripes, spoilers and new rims, she is one of a kind like me!

My Next Goal

All of my children are grown as well as my husband's. I'm ready to leave our current home to move to Poland. Plans were in the works to buy an apartment close to his dad's place, but **Tato** has since passed away, leaving us the apartment my husband grew up in. Friends he went to school with are close by. We are absolutely amped for this move.

Now that I write full time, I will fulfill my childhood dream. To write and travel.

Conclusion

Now that you have read some basic information on the Law of Attraction and learned some beginner manifesting techniques, you should be ready to begin your journey towards making your dreams and desires a reality. Think of something that you have always wanted; even if it seems out of reach. Are you renting a small apartment in the city, but yearn for a house of your own with a yard for the dog that you have always wanted? Material things are an excellent focus that can bring you great happiness when they materialize. Are you stuck in a dead-end job that you dread going to every day and wish you could successfully start your own business? Striving for success is another great focus that can be achieved through manifesting if you genuinely believe it will happen for you. Are you single after a string of bad relationships and are just unsure whether you will find a significant other with whom you share common interests? Manifesting can help with your love life and bring the right person into your life, often in the most unexpected way. Have you been hoping to lose that last twenty pounds, but just haven't been able to stay motivated enough to reach your goal weight? You can even manifest fitness and health with the Law of Attraction, but it is up to you to bring the things you are seeking into reality.

Begin with a vision board so that you have a physical representation of the things that you want. This will make it easier to maintain focus. As you focus daily on your dreams, keep a clear mind, and watch out for blocks and mistakes that you may be making. It is best to catch them early so that you learn how to avoid them quickly. Don't be discouraged if you have a slow start. As with all things, you need to practice before you can achieve the results you want. Many people want too many things too fast but fail to realize them because the universe couldn't get a clear message of what they were seeking. Even if you start small, success may find you sooner than you think. While it may be slow to start, keep believing, and send out the message to the universe that you know that success will happen for you. Keep your intentions pure and positive so that the universe is receiving your message clearly. What the universe gives is up to you because it will return what it is given. As long as you truly believe, then you will find success and achieve it!

References

Bodian, S. (2006). Meditation for Dummies (2nd Ed.). Wiley Publishing, Inc.

Byrne, R. (2006). The Secret. Atria Books.

The Big Book of Personal Affirmations and Mantras. (2011). DawnPublishing.

Hurst, K. (2019, April 02). Celebrities and the Law of Attraction Success Stories. The Law of Attraction. Retrieved October 02, 2020, from https://www.thelawofattraction.com/celebrities-law-attraction/

Jacobs, C. (2010). Detox for the Rest of Us: Safe and Easy Plans to Cleanse Your Body, Boost Your Metabolism, Lose Weight, and Feel Great! F+W Media, Inc.

Losier, M. J. (2007) Law of Attraction: The Science of Attracting More of What You Want and Less of What You Don't. Wellness Central.

Malone, G. (2018). The Essence of Reiki. Gerry-Malone.com Limited.

Morris, J. (2011). The Ultimate Vision Board Guide. Jayne Morris—Power-Up Coaching.

Shaw, A. (2014). Mastering the Law of Attraction. Andy Shaw.

References

Wörle, L. & Pfeiff, E. (2010). Yoga as Therapeutic Exercise: A Practical Guide for Manual Therapists. Elsevier Ltd.

About the Author

Monique Joiner Siedlak is a writer, witch, and warrior on a mission to awaken people to their greatest potential through the power of storytelling infused with mysticism, modern paganism, and new age spirituality. At the young age of 12, she began rigorously studying the fascinating philosophy of Wicca. By the time she was 20, she was self-initiated into the craft, and hasn't looked back ever since. To this day, she has authored over 40 books pertaining to the magick and mysteries of life.

To find out more about Monique Joiner Siedlak artistically, spiritually, and personally, feel free to visit her **official website**.

www.mojosiedlak.com

 facebook.com/mojosiedlak

 twitter.com/mojosiedlak

 instagram.com/mojosiedlak

 pinterest.com/mojosiedlak

 bookbub.com/authors/monique-joiner-siedlak

Other Books by the Author

African Magic

Hoodoo

Seven African Powers: The Orishas

Cooking For the Orishas

Lucumi: The Ways of Santeria

Voodoo of Louisiana

Practical Magick

Wiccan Basics

Candle Magick

Wiccan Spells

Love Spells

Abundance Spells

Herb Magick

Moon Magick

Creating Your Own Spells

Gypsy Magic

The Yoga Collective

Yoga for Beginners

Yoga for Stress

Yoga for Back Pain

Yoga for Weight Loss

Yoga for Flexibility

Yoga for Advanced Beginners

Yoga for Fitness

Yoga for Runners

Yoga for Energy

Yoga for Your Sex Life

Yoga to Beat Depression and Anxiety

Yoga for Menstruation

Yoga to Detox Your Body

Toga to Tone Your Body

A Natural Beautiful You

Creating Your Own Body Butter

Creating Your Own Body Scrub

Creating Your Own Body Spray

Last Chance
Join My Newsletter!

If you missed it, I have a free gift available for you and wanted to remind you it's still available.

mojosiedlak.com/self-help-and-yoga-newsletter

Thank you for reading my book.
I really appreciate all your feedback and would love to hear what you have to say!
Please leave your review at your favorite retailer!

Thank you